TRAUMA OF CHANGE WORKBOOK

Proofread by Diahann Ogunde

DISCLAIMER AND COPYRIGHT NOTICE

This disclaimer applies to each reader of The Trauma of Change System Workbook. While the information contained within this workbook is believed to be accurate, no guarantee is given that the information provided in this workbook is correct or complete.

The materials contained in this workbook are provided for general information purposes only and do not constitute medical, legal, or other professional advice on any subject matter, nor are they meant for use as medical diagnosis or replacement of medical advice. Elite International Coaching, LLC won't accept any responsibility for any loss which may arise from reliance on information contained in this program. Although the methods suggested in this workbook reflect an **evidence-based** process to rewire the brain for meaningful life changes and creating shifts in brain circuitry, there are no guarantees of success associated with the use of this workbook as individual results may vary according to the application, and such claim is not under the control of the author. The contents of this workbook are protected by copyright under international conventions. No material within this workbook may be reproduced for commercial purposes.

This workbook and its contents are provided "AS IS" without warranty of any kind, either express or implied, including, but not limited to, the implied warranties of merchantability, fitness for a particular purpose, or non-infringement. Use of this workbook is done at the user's own risk.

Reproduction, distribution, republication, and/or retransmission of material contained within this workbook are prohibited unless the prior written permission of Elite International Coaching, LLC, a Georgia State corporation, has been obtained. For further terms and conditions, please see the full disclaimer at https://www. reneecharles.com.

Table of Contents

Introduction 1
1   Neurotheology and Trauma 2
2   The Trauma of Change System Model™ 3
3   Trauma Wounds & Bruises 4
4   Trauma of Change Wound Healing 11
5   Trauma of Change Triage Processing Phase 12
6   Phases of Physiologic Wound Healing 16
7   Spiritual Portals - Evicting Demonic Squatters 18
8   Trauma of Change - Deliverance Stage Processing Phase 22
9   Trauma of Change - Stage Processing Healing Phases 25
10 Trauma of Change - Recovery Stage Processing 27
11 Trauma of Change - Steps to Rewire the Brain 29
12 Psychological Properties of Colors 42
13 Resources Page 62
14 TOC Survey Questionnaire 63
15 Appendix: The Salvation Confession 42
16 Bonus Quiz 62

Introduction

I am pleased to provide this companion to my book entitled *Remembering the Trauma*. *The Trauma of Change Workbook* is both an instructional guide and a self-help system. The Trauma of Change System Model™ (TOC) outlined in *Remembering the Trauma* is presented with action steps to facilitate transformative deliverance and healing by understanding the mind-body-brain connection.

Trauma happens to us all: friends, colleagues, families, and neighbors. Counseling helps to develop coping skills but usually does not help the traumatized to become free. You can restructure the circuitry of your brain by superimposing the Word of God over terrorizing memories and take authority over what has kept you captive. The Trauma of Change System Model™ (when all action steps and suggested activities in faith and prayer are followed as outlined) may have a positive life-altering effect for the reader.

The nexus between healing, deliverance, and recovery is a dynamic one that requires a dual focus to eradicate the memory of traumatic events. The spirit of trauma affects brain circuitry. This often leaves victims of trauma disabled with terrorizing memories. The good news is, according to research, one can rewire the brain and rebuild areas affected by trauma.

1 | NEUROTHEOLOGY AND TRAUMA

Neurotheology, also known as spiritual neuroscience, attempts to explain religious experience and behavior in neuroscientific terms. Trauma healing and recovery is an evolving process affected by the optimization of brain function.

People who have been traumatized hold an implicit memory of traumatic events in their brains and bodies. Through these memories, the devil can infiltrate the mind of believers with feelings of shame and guilt about their past and present lives.

The trauma of childhood neglect, abandonment, rejection, betrayal, and sexual abuse can wreak havoc in the body; and create strongholds in one or more of its 11 systems. Trauma disrupts the stress-hormone system and causes havoc within the nervous system. These disruptions prevent people from processing and integrating traumatic memories into conscious mental frameworks.

Strongholds and Trauma
Behind every stronghold, there is a framework of trauma incapacitating believers from manifesting the glory of God in their lives. Deliverance and healing begin initially in our minds.

We must affirm and believe in our hearts that Jesus healed the brokenhearted, delivered the captives from bondage and fear, recovered sight to the blind, and set at liberty them that are bruised. To fully experience the benefit and victory afforded to man by the finished work of Christ, I invite you to accept Jesus Christ as your Lord and Savior today. Accepting Christ is as simple as A-B-C. Read the steps in the resource section and email me to celebrate your decision to become victorious in Him.

2 | THE TRAUMA OF CHANGE SYSTEM MODEL™

The Trauma of Change System Model™ (TOC), conceptualized by the author under the leading of the Holy Spirit, is a faith-based recovery process and system/approach designed to systematically repair brain function after a traumatic assault, improve higher-order brain activity, facilitate deliverance from traumatizing memories, thereby promoting healing and recovery.

The TOC System Model integrates the best of neuroscience, psychology, physiology, neurotheology, and Biblio-technology. It has a concentrated focus on core spiritual states of healing, deliverance, and recovery.

The Model begins with the philosophy that healing, deliverance, and recovery is a choice decision. Medical research reveals that you heal from a disease, but you recover from an illness. The disease can be mental, spiritual or physical. Healing is a choice and a decision which involves a shift in the energy generated by conscious and unconscious processes.

It is critical to remember that trauma wound healing is not linear; healing can progress both forwards and back through the phases depending on intrinsic and extrinsic motivational forces.

3 | TRAUMA WOUNDS & BRUISES

Early experiences involving neglect, emotional, sexual or physical abuse, random domestic violence, and repeated abandonment create deep wounds in the soul. These wounds can be long-lasting. For instance, trauma wounds and bruises inflicted during the early developmental years can cause children to become adults who disregard or distrust their emotions and even their bodies. Just as natural wounds can differ in severity, injuries resulting from an emotional trauma also vary in severity.

Taking God-inspired liberty, the medical definition of natural wounds is outlined to contextualize the mirror image of an injury to the soul based on the Trauma of Change System Model™.

Physical Wounds
There are six types of open wounds to the body.[1] Each wound is classified by its cause. Synonymous with the word injury are such terms as a lesion, cut, gash, laceration, tear, slash, graze, scratch, abrasion, bruise, or contusion. Some trauma wounds are minor and can be treated with over-the-counter first aid. Other injuries require more than a first-aid approach to prevent infection, organ failure, and ultimately the loss of life.

Soul Wounds
Just as natural wounds can differ in severity, soul wound resulting from an emotional trauma also vary in severity. Taking God-inspired liberty, the medical definition of a physical wound is henceforth contrasted with an emotional wound in the realm of the spirit to demonstrate what the injury to the soul would look like.

Open Wounds
An open wound is created in the natural when there is an external or internal break (more than a half-inch) of skin to living tissue.[2] The skin is the first surface layer of protection. With this kind of wound, the bleeding does not stop by merely applying direct pressure to the wound. If the bleeding lasts longer than 20 minutes, the injury will result in severe trauma to the body.

---

[1] https://www.livestrong.com/article/101274-five-types-wounds/
[2] https://medical-dictionary.thefreedictionary.com/open+wound

Penetrating Wound Trauma

Penetrating trauma is an injury that occurs when an object pierces the skin and enters a tissue of the body creating an open wound. The penetrating object may remain in the tissue, come back out the way entered or pass through the membranes and exit from another area.[3]

Penetrating trauma can be severe because it can damage internal organs and it presents a risk of shock and infection.

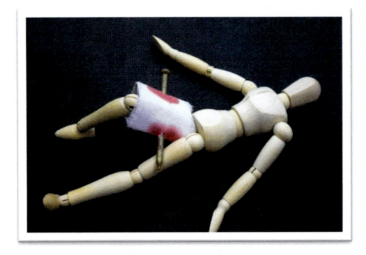

Illustration 1 Source[4]

---

[3] https://www.definitions.net/definition/penetrating trauma
[4] en.wikipedia.org/wiki/Perforating trauma

Perforating Wound Trauma

Illustration 2 Source[5]

Perforating trauma is an injury usually occurring accidentally or intentionally—as in a violent crime. A perforating injury is associated with an entrance wound and often more massive exit wound where an object enters the body and moves all the way through the skin.[6]

Dysfunctional Behaviors: The Perforating Soul Wound

Penetrating and perforating trauma can damage internal organs resulting in dysfunctional behaviors such as substance abuse, mental illness, prostitution, low self-esteem and toxic binding relationships. Penetrating trauma leaves noticeable wounds indexed by fear, anxiety, and distrust of people, places and things.

---

[5] https://stock.adobe.com/license
[6] en.wikipedia.org/wiki/Perforating trauma

Abrasions

Illustration 3 Source[7]

Abrasion occurs when the skin rubs or scrapes against a rough or hard exterior.[8] There's usually not much bleeding, but the wound needs to be scrubbed and cleaned to avoid infection.

Internalized Anger: The Abrasion Soul Wound

Abrasions in the soul can be likened to the daily manifestation of uncontrolled anger (rage) about the victimization and hostile response to an egregious injury. Anger is a natural response to the failure of others to meet one's needs for love, praise, and acceptance. Internalized anger may be masked as repressed fear upheld by intimidating secrets, co-occurring with shame and or guilt.

Incisions

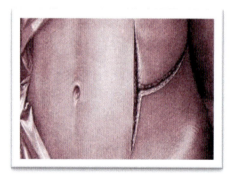

Illustration 4 Source[9]

An incision is a cut, or a wound made by a sharp instrument or object, such as a knife, shard of glass, or razor blade. Incisions bleed a lot and very quickly. A deep incision can damage tendons, ligaments, and muscles.[10]

---

[7] https://stock.adobe.com/license
[8] https://medical-dictionary.thefreedictionary.com/Abrasions
[9] https://medical-dictionary.thefreedictionary.com/incised+wound
[10] ibid

Betrayal: The Incision Soul Wound

An incision wound in the soul is akin to betrayal trauma. Betrayal trauma impairs a person's self-concept and bleeds into every area of self-care, in particular, establishing trust and maintaining meaningful relationships.

Betrayal trauma is defined as a trauma perpetrated by someone with whom the victim is close to and reliant upon for support and survival.

Traumatic experiences involving a betrayal of trust, particularly childhood abuse, can cause severe suffering, impair daily functioning, increase the risk of further victimization and perpetration of violence, and create different mental health and societal problems (Freyd, DePrince, & Zurbriggen, 2001, p. 6)[11].

Laceration

Illustration 5 Source[12]

A laceration is a deep cut or tearing of the skin. Accidents with knives, tools, and machinery frequently are the cause of a laceration or gash. The bleeding is rapid and extensive, requiring knitting of the flesh to stop the profuse bleeding.[13]

Soul Ties: The Laceration Soul Wound

This type of wound is akin to a soul tie with the spirit of perversion and/or addiction to people, things, and places. A soul tie occurs when two souls are knitted together as one flesh in the spiritual realm. Soul ties and co-dependency occur typically when ignored, shamed, or punished for expressing thoughts or feelings or for being immature, imperfect, or having needs and wants.

---

[11] Freyd, J. J., DePrince, A. P., & Zurbriggen, E. L. (2001). Self-reported memory for abuse depends upon victim-perpetrator relationship. Journal of Trauma & Dissociation, 2, 5-17.
[12] https://www.healthline.com/health/open-wound
[13] ibid

Lacerations are the realm of the spirit may result in psychological dysfunctions such as diagnosis of bipolar disorder and other personality type disorders.

Puncture Wound

A puncture is a small hole caused by a long, pointy object, such as a nail, needle, or ice pick. Puncture wounds may not bleed much but can be broad enough to damage internal organs.

Illustration 6 Sourc [14]

Childhood Abandonment: The Puncture Soulish Wound

A puncture wound to the soul is akin to childhood abandonment. This type of wounding is similar to childhood abandonment and/or neglect which is one of the highest forms of abuse.

In the United States of America, neglect accounts for 78 percent of all child maltreatment cases, far more than physical abuse (17 percent), sexual abuse (9 percent), and psychological abuse (8 percent) combined.[15] Science tells us that young children who experience significantly limited caregiver responsiveness may sustain a range of adverse physical and mental health consequences that actually produce more widespread developmental impairments than overt physical abuse.[16] These can include cognitive delays, stunting of physical growth, impairments in executive function and self-regulation skills, and disruptions of the body's stress response.[17]

Early-life trauma affects future self-esteem, social awareness, ability to learn and physical health. When the attachment bond goes well, neurological integration usually develops, and relationships bring the expectation of safety, appreciation, joy, and pleasure. A lack of nurturing by the parent(s) results in the child feeling starved for affection to fill the emptiness felt. If the attachment bond were unsuccessful and traumatizing, neural dysregulation and memories of a failed relationship would become the basis for adult expectations of intimacy.[18]

---

[14] *https://stock.adobe.com* (under license)
[15] https://www.outofkit.com
[16] https://developingchild.harvard.edu/science/deep-dives/neglect/
[17] ibid
[18] Taxonomy of Trauma and Trauma Assessment Ibrahim Aref Kira (n.d.). Source: from
 https://www.myptsd.com/gallery/-pdf/1-88.pdf

Avulsions

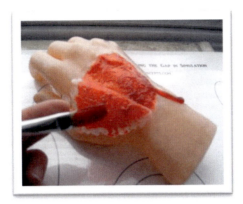

Illustration 7 Source[19]

An avulsion is a trauma wound which involves a complete tearing away of skin or tissue from a body structure. Avulsions may result from trauma or surgery. Avulsions usually occur during violent accidents, such as body-crushing accidents, explosions, and gunshots. The wound bleeds massively and rapidly.[20]

The Avulsion Soul Wound: Low Self-Esteem

An avulsion wound may be likened to the emotional life-altering trauma wounds to the soul that affect esteem. Traumas, such as rape, incest, and sexual abuse tear away at self-esteem and cause distrust of the world. If the tear in the emotional tissue remains undressed, it can last for a lifetime.

---

[19] https://www.healthline.com/health/open-wound
[20] https://www.revolvy.com/page/Avulsion-injury

4 | TRAUMA OF CHANGE WOUND HEALING

Healing is a part of salvation available through the death and resurrection of Jesus Christ. Divine healing ministers to our physical, emotional, and mental sickness. Trauma healing is God in action. Healing and recovery are a restorative process of regaining possession or control of something stolen or lost to return one to a former and better state of wholeness.

We understand now that often behind a stronghold, a framework of trauma is hidden. The spirit of trauma found an entrance into the soul and established a foothold or stronghold. The strongholds must be disabled and forbidden to gain entry again. In the realm of the Spirit, the initial phase of healing can manifest when you triage the injury by superimposing the Word of God over low-level disabling negative thoughts. Understanding the spiritual wound types is an essential step in knowing how to apply the steps outlined in the stage processing phase of deliverance. By neutralizing the frequency of negative thoughts, you will provide a locus of control over that which is attempting to control you. As in the natural, wound triage requires different approaches and post-surgery monitoring to advance the healing process. Your cells will respond to everything that you say or think. The WORD of God and His promises found in scripture are constructive, growth-oriented, and fueling. The Word of God will build new thought patterns, release endorphins, strengthen your immune system, and facilitate healing.

Healing is the body's natural process of repairing damage caused by physical or mental trauma and is the method of combating the disease. The initial triage of a wound is followed by treatment which also may include surgery and aftercare. Some physical wounds are minor and can, therefore, respond to minimal treatment with an over-the-counter first aid approach. Steps for treating natural wounds can be retrofitted to the first phase of triaging an emotional trauma wound.

5 | TRAUMA OF CHANGE TRIAGE PROCESSING PHASE

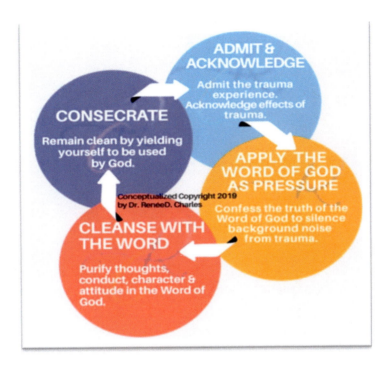

1. **Wound Triage - First Step:** Admit that the trauma experience happened, and that the memories still torment you. Rate your experience of trauma on a scale of 1 to 5 with the lowest score being 1.

How intrusive is the memory of the trauma experienced?

_____
_____
_____
_____
_____
_____
_____
_____
_____
_____

The Trauma of Change System Model™

*Write the thoughts that you have about it **today**.*

_____
_____
_____
_____
_____
_____
_____
_____
_____

Check the wound type(s) that resonate most with you. Record your answer in the score sheet found in the resource segment of the workbook.

- ☐ Penetrating
- ☐ Incision
- ☐ Abrasion
- ☐ Avulsions
- ☐ Perforating
- ☐ Puncture

2. **Wound Triage - Second Step**: Remove any debris or object remaining on the surface or embedded in the skin. If the object is large or deeply embedded in the skin or muscle, removing it may cause additional injury. Likewise, attempts made to mentally disassociate from memory (or deny the trauma event) will manifest in behavioral forms.

Clean and protect the wound. Wash and disinfect it with water to remove all dirt and debris. Water is the universal solvent and symbolic of the Holy Spirit. God provides water to the thirsty (John 14:14). There is water in God's Word. In Ephesians 5:26, the apostle Paul tells us that we are cleansed "with the washing of water by the word." When we study the Word and declare the Word; it purifies our thoughts, conduct, character, and attitudes.

Imagine that you are cleaning the debris in and surrounding the trauma wound. Are there any objects that are still embedded? If yes, what steps will you take to remove the debris?

_____

_____

_____

_____

_____

On a scale of 1 to 5 with five being the most positive action to remove debris, rate the action you would take. _____

The action I will take to remove trauma debris is:

_____

_____

_____

_____

_____

3. **Wound Triage - Third Step**: Apply firm, direct pressure and elevate the wound. Applying pressure will control the bleeding and swelling. Continue to use force with a sterile gauze or clean cloth until the bleeding stops.

Spiritually, this application of pressure is like the instruction in Hebrews 10:23 to "hold tightly without wavering to the hope we affirm, for God can be trusted to keep his promise" (New Living Translation). Holding tightly to the promises of God for total healing drowns out the background noise that is struggling to be in first place position.

What do you believe you could have done differently (if anything) in response to the trauma experienced?

_____
_____
_____
_____
_____

4. ***Wound Triage Fourth Step: Wrap the Wound.*** Wrapping the wound keeps it from being exposed to germs. Just as we must close natural wounds with a sterile dressing, we must embrace what the Word of God says in Leviticus 20:7: "Sanctify yourselves, therefore, and be ye holy: for I am the Lord your God" (King James Version).

Keep the trauma wound clean and dry by consecrating yourself to the Lord. You can do this by simply just saying, "Lord Jesus, I am for You. I'm no longer for myself, the world, or anything else. I am for Your use and Your satisfaction."

What phase of healing would you say that you are in?

☐ Homeostasis ☐ Inflammatory

☐ Proliferative ☐ Remodeling

On a scale of 1 to 5 with five being the highest, rated score How likely are you to facilitate the next phase of healing? _____

Record your answer in the resource segment of the workbook.

6 | PHASES OF PHYSIOLOGIC WOUND HEALING

In the natural realm, wound healing is the physiologic restoration of structure and function of injured or diseased tissues.[21] The healing processes include blood clotting, tissue mending, scarring, and bone healing.

Wound healing is a complex process of biochemical reactions and cellular events in which the skin, and the tissues under it repair themselves after injury. When a person experiences physical trauma, the skin—as the largest organ in the body—activates wound healing. The Four Phases of Wound Healing are 1st - Homeostasis; 2nd - Inflammation; 3rd - Proliferation; and 4th - Remodeling.

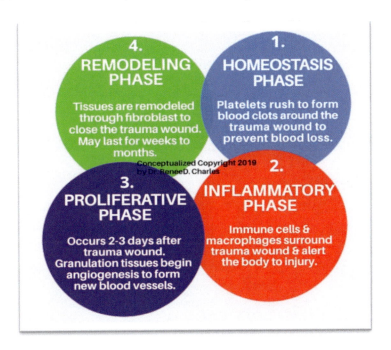

Natural Progress of Wound Healing

1. ***The Homeostasis Phase*** is the first phase of wound healing. Platelets—blood cells that are critical in forming clots—aggregate at the damaged site and initiate clot formation to prevent blood loss and create a temporary covering that protects the area from the external environment.

2. ***Inflammatory Phase*** is the second phase and the body's natural response to injury. While the platelets aggregate, they also secrete factors that recruit other immune cells. These factors initiate the inflammatory phase. Inflammation is your body's way of alerting you of an injury.

---

[21] https://www.ncbi.nlm.nih.gov/pubmed/11074996

The Trauma of Change System Model™

After initial wounding, the blood vessels in the wound bed contract and form a clot. The next wave of immune cells to arrive at the scene includes monocytes and can be mobilized in response to injury or infection. Once in the wound, these cells can differentiate into cells called macrophages, the immune system's "construction workers."

Imagine yourself as the architect of your body. Envision the cells of your body as "construction workers" ready to facilitate healing. Write the name of your team of "construction workers" below. Provide a work order below to construct wound repair.

_____

_____

_____

_____

_____

Rate your experience of trauma on a scale of 1 to 5.
How do you rank your emotional healing from trauma? _____

3. The Proliferative Phase: Rebuilding

The Proliferative Phase is the third phase of wound healing and resolves the inflammatory phase. The Proliferative Phase occurs two to three days after the injury and is the period where the wound contracts as new tissues are rebuilt.

During *proliferation*, the wound is 'rebuilt' with new granulation tissue. The granulation tissue is comprised of collagen and extracellular matrix. New blood vessels are formed through angiogenesis. These vessels become a new network. Once the bleeding is under control, the body then begins the process of rebuilding tissue.

Looking back, how well equipped do you feel to handle any wound bleeds? Use the scale of 1 to 5 to record your answer to the survey questions in the resource section of the workbook.

4. The Remodeling phase is the final stage that occurs once the wound has closed and involves tissue remodeling by fibroblasts, which can persist for weeks to months. Although the wound is closed at this point, the tissue is not entirely back to normal. Granulation tissue typically grows from the base of a wound and can fill wounds of almost any size. Its production and the swift wound closure that accompanied it are merely stopgap measures to prevent blood loss and infection.

7 | SPIRITUAL PORTALS – EVICTING DEMONIC SQUATTERS

Parallel portals exist both in the natural and spiritual realms. A spiritual portal is a doorway, gate, or entryway that allows bi-directional access from the physical world to the spirit world. Bacteria enter our bodies through internal or external surface points that are damaged or compromised due to cuts, scrapes or other wounds. Similarly, the enemy looks for access points to gain footholds into the soul.

In the spiritual or supernatural realm, a traumatic event can provide demonic spirits with legal or illegal access to one or more of the body chambers. The human body has many entry and exit portals. The ears, eyes, nose, mouth, skin, anus, urethra, cervix, sexual organs, and mammary glands are all entry and exit portals that demonic spirits can access.

Evicting Demonic Squatters

Demonic spirits travel in groups. They can access one or more of the 11 systems within the body. These demons, hereto referred to as demonic squatters, can enter the human body by open invitation or illegal entry. Upon entry, demons establish "squatter's rights" and become lodged in one or more physical organs. Once lodged in the body and spirit, demonic squatters can continue bruising, wounding and terrorizing their host.

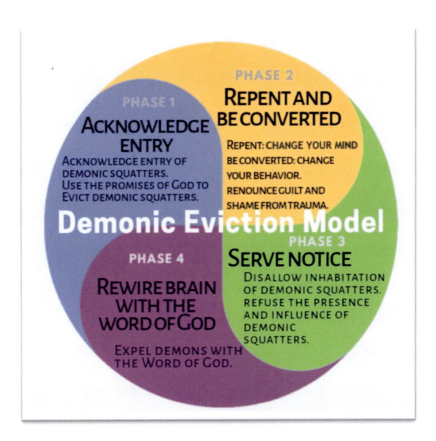

Step 1: Acknowledge Entry

The first step to dislodge demonic squatters is to acknowledge their illegal or legal entry into your life. Satan has legal authority on earth as a result of Adam's forfeiture of dominion in the earth, but Jesus has come so that we may have life and have it more abundantly. By the authority given to you as a joint heir with Jesus Christ, you can access His power and promises on earth to evict demonic squatters.

In the book *Remembering the Trauma*, details about access to the soul by demonic squatters is detailed.

On the scale of 1 to 5 how likely was access to your soul by demonic squatters obtained legally directly or indirectly? _____

Step 2: Repent and Be Converted

The second step is to repent and be converted. Regardless of whether legal access was granted to demonic squatters or if they entered illegally, the next step is to repent unto God. Repentance is "an inward decision or change of mind resulting in the outward action of turning from sin to God and righteousness" Acts 20:21 (KJV). Conversion is the change in thinking and behavior that follows repentance. After you repent and are converted, you must repeatedly renounce feelings of guilt and shame related to the trauma. When repentance is linked to conversion, the spirit of trauma will leave as you resist him and join the Kingdom of God.

If you are saved, write your repentance prayer below.

_____
_____
_____
_____
_____

If you have not yet surrendered your life to the Lord. Salvation is available now!

The traumatizing event sent to you by satan were attempts to separate you from God, weaken your body, damage relationships, disrupt healthy thought patterns and to drive you into despair. Perhaps, you have been under the effects of trauma until now.

Healing is immediately available to you if you embrace it. You've already made the decision to choose deliverance by reading the book *Remembering the Trauma*. You don't have to suffer from traumatic memories and strongholds. The penalty of sin has already been paid by Jesus. You need not to be in a church or religious setting to receive salvation.

Let's take the next step of salvation together. Salvation is as simple as A-B-C. Please see the resource section for a detailed salvation prayer.

"If you declare with your mouth, "Jesus is Lord," and believe in your heart that God raised him from the dead, you will be saved. For it is with your heart that you believe and are justified, and it is with your mouth that you profess your faith in Jesus Christ and are saved" Rom. 10:9-10 (New International Version).

Step 3: Serve Notice

The third step is to serve notice to the demonic squatters that you disallow their habitation in the name of Jesus and forbid any further encroachment in your life. The Holy Spirit is the discerner of truth. The brain is the central processing unit. As you refuse to tolerate the presence and influence of demonic squatters, you shall know the truth, and the truth shall set you free (John 8:32).

Write the eviction notice in your own words.

_____

_____

_____

_____

_____

When you are writing something down with a pen and paper, you are stimulating a collection of cells in the base of your brain known as the Reticular Activating System. The RAS is the filter for all information that your brain needs to process, and it gives more attention to what you are currently focusing on. The physical act of writing brings the information to the forefront and triggers your *brain to pay close attention. The part of the brain that is associated with* **speaking** *and* **writing** *is the frontal lobe.*

This area is also responsible for movement, reasoning, judgment, planning, and problem-solving. The parietal lobe is also important in writing. This part of the brain interprets words and language.

Refer to the warfare prayer of Archbishop William Duncan located in the appendix of the *Remembering the Trauma Book.* Use the full arsenal of ammunition at your disposal.

The enemy wants your mind. There is a **difference between** the mind and the brain. The brain is an organ made up of physical matter, but the mind isn't. The brain is the physical place that the mind resides. It is a vessel in which electronic impulses that create thought is contained. It is the limitless source that regulates the flow of energy within the brain. The **brain** is made up of cells, blood vessels and nerves to name a few. **Mind** is nothing but the thought that resides in the **brain**. The brain takes the shape that the mind rests on. Watch your thoughts. Any thought that does not line up with the Word of God must be cast down within 30 seconds or it will become a stronghold.

Step 4: Rewire Your Brain with the Word of God

The **fourth step** is to rewire your brain using the Word of God. You can expel demons and rewire your brain by renewing your mind with the Word of God. Romans 12:2 explains how you can be transformed by the renewing of your mind. Satan's demons cannot share space with the Word of God in a vessel that is saved, sanctified, and submitted to Him.

Review the 10 steps outlined in the "Rewire Your Brain" section of the workbook. Following the TOC System, incorporate additional strategies at will. The rewiring system approach involves intentional activities to restrict damage to areas of the brain to develop neural mental map pathways and evict demonic squatters.

8 | TRAUMA OF CHANGE - DELIVERANCE STAGE PROCESSING PHASE

Deliverance is a multifaceted process and not a one-time visit to the altar. The second stage processing segment of the Trauma of Change Faith-Based Model™ focuses on facilitating deliverance in the lives of victims of trauma.

Although healing and deliverance are somewhat different, they are relational because of the triune nature of man. Deliverance is the process of dismantling demonic strongholds which create psychological and physical diseases. It deals with demonically caused mental and physical conditions. Deliverance from demonic forces must begin in your mind and be manifested by the words you release from your mouth.

Humanity is a speaking spirit. God is complemented when we behave and speak like Him. Your speech is the first line of defense against the spirit of trauma. Accessing the truth of the Word of God will catapult the person into the next stage processing of trauma healing. You must speak words of declaration in alignment with the Word of God to take authority over your body.

The Trauma of Change System Model™

Words matter. Words create life and death (Proverbs 18:21). Your mind, your cells, and your faith all respond to every word that you say or think. If you change how you feel based on the Word of God, you will change how you speak. Speech is the conduit of thought. As your level of thinking (your ideas) are upgraded, your level of expression (your speech—words released out of your mouth) will be enhanced. The higher the order of thinking, the higher the level of thought; and the higher and greater the outcome will be. Victorious healing is attainable when declarations are made over the body in alignment with the Word of God. Words are symbolic of thought.

However, without context, words have no meaning. In the Bible, deliverance refers to the acts of God, whereby He rescues His people from their enemies. God has varied methods of deliverance to rescue (save) His people.

In **1 Samuel 17:37 and 2 Kings 20:6, deliverance is symbolized as a "snatch away"** from the hand of the wicked.

In **Psalm 7:2; 17:13; 18:16-19; 59:2; 69:14; and 71:4, deliverance is symbolized to "make an escape;" "cause to escape;" "draw out;" and "to save"** God's people from danger.

In the New Testament Gospels, Jesus commissioned His disciples to preach the Gospel with the commandment—to always minister healing and deliverance. He told them "As you go heal the sick, cast out demons" (Matt. 10:1, 7-8).

The **initial stage processing** *phase of deliverance* involves a self-examination of the individual need for deliverance. Making decisions includes creating intentions and setting goals. These activities are all part of the same neural circuitry and positively engage the prefrontal cortex, which reduces worry and anxiety.

A person changes their thinking about a thing when new evidence appears that contradicts and challenges their belief system. Unresolved traumas intertwined with dysfunctional beliefs can hinder the deliverance healing and recovery process, resulting in psychopathology.

The **second stage processing** *phase of deliverance* processing is repentance and conversion. Repentance is an inward decision or change of mind resulting in the outward action of turning from sin to God and righteousness. See Act 21:20. The Biblical definition of repentance means to shift from the wrong way to the right direction.

Repentance and conversion are followed by a repeated renunciation of feelings of guilt and shame related to trauma. When repentance is linked to conversion, the individual will leave the kingdom of satan and join the Kingdom of God.

The **third stage processing** *phase of deliverance* locates and shuts all portal doors that were open generationally and or willingly allowing legal or illegal access to the temple. You close open doors by sealing them permanently by rededicating your life to one of holiness coupled with warfare declaration prays. Unless you close those doors, the devil has a legal right to steal, kill and destroy any blessing that is in their life.

The **fourth stage processing** *phase of deliverance* involves evicting demonic squatters from your earthly temple to be set free from the spirit of trauma. You will have to decide to see yourself free and confess the truth of the Word that you already have eternal victory over satan and demonic spirits through Jesus Christ.

"Sanctify yourselves, therefore, and be ye holy: for I am the Lord your God. And ye shall keep my statutes, and do them: I am the Lord which sanctify you" Lev. 20:7-8 (KJV).

Sanctification is separation from the seduction of sin involving the restoration or salvation of the soul. Repentance and conversion result in justification and salvation, sanctification and glorification. The process of justification is separation from the penalty of sin involving the re-creation of the spirit. When you are justified by repentance and conversion, you are "saved" from a life of sin as well as from the penalties of sin.

9 | TRAUMA OF CHANGE - STAGE PROCESSING HEALING PHASES

Emotional trauma wounds require more than a first-aid approach to forestall demonic encroachment and dismantle the foul ground. When you possess an unshakable mentality and prevailing belief that you are no longer a victim but victorious through Jesus Christ, you can safely transition into the first processing phase of trauma healing.

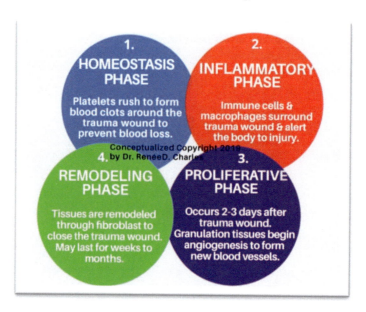

The Flooding Stage is the spiritual **Homeostasis Phase** and the *first processing phase of a trauma wound healing.* In this stage, words of truth surround the trauma experience to start the process of trauma wound treatment and healing. Words of truth are critical in forming growth-oriented thoughts, which build and fuel the healing process.

Water begins to seek its level. Fragments of the trauma memory start to rapidly pool and aggregate around a single trauma event in response to memories rehearsed and words released into the atmosphere. To forestall and prevent memory rehearsal, you will have to create a temporary shield. This shield is made of affirming words of truth and prevents demons from occupying mental space with lies. When affirming words are superimposed in opposition to the trauma, the truth provides a level of protection from the inner voices and the external environment.

The Replay Stage is the spiritual **Inflammatory Phase** and the *second processing phase of a trauma wound healing.* In the Replay Stage, the spirit of trauma replays the traumatic memory scene. Every mental replay recruits other fragmented elements unrelated to the trauma event, which stirs negative emotions and triggers emotional inflammation. Trauma memories intertwine and heap feelings of doubt, confusion, and depression on the person. Feelings of shame and guilt emerge in this stage.

During the Replay Stage, demonic voices are attempting to penetrate and destroy the shield of words of truth, which was erected during the First Flooding Stage. Demonic squatters need the foundation of lies and deceit to continue to occupy ground. However, God's angels are on assignment and are on your side. Angels serve as "first responders" and rush to reinforce the shield of affirming words of truth to prohibit any further encroachment.

The Mental Shift Stage (which is the **Spiritual Proliferative Phase**) occurs between the two to three days immediately after the trauma event has occurred and is the *third processing phase of a trauma wound healing*. The start of the Mental Shift Stage resolves the **Inflammatory Phase** and ends the period where dominant thoughts emerge from the soul and continuously replay the trauma incident.

During Mental Shift, the matrix of the trauma memory is converted from negative to positive. As the mind changes, the brain changes. The Mental Shift begins to create a new neural network to equip the individual with more effective ways to think, feel, and respond to the trauma memories.

You can use your mind to create new habits! Through the repeated actions of applying the Word of God, the connections of new, healthy thoughts create new mental or neural pathways which become established and stronger. With continuous practice and training, you can rewire your neural pathways according to the habits and memories you want to create.

The Confession Phase is the spiritual **Remodeling Phase** and the *final processing phase of a trauma wound healing*. Once new neuropathways are established, the trauma memory undergoes permanent remodeling as new mental maps are created. The Confession Phase can persist from weeks to months.

This final Confession Stage involves confession of sins of omission and/or commission. Such purposeful and indirect acts may have afforded demonic access to soul encroachment (access to the soul)—whether legal or illegal. In the Proliferative Phase, the defense shield created by enforcing it with the Word of God, if done hastily and with an unrepentant heart, will only serve as an emergency stopgap. The truth must be reinforced to become permanent. Without confession, the other preceding stage processes are only temporary, and eventually, the individual will regress and be overwhelmed by tormenting trauma memories.

10 | TRAUMA OF CHANGE - RECOVERY STAGE PROCESSING

In concert with the TOC philosophy, we embrace the concept that *recovery* is a process of spiritual development and growth that involves the whole person. Recovery is an evolving process beginning with a readiness to examine and discard self-defeating beliefs and behaviors. The TOC model foundational concept essentially is that Recovery is a God-directed, self-help process influenced by a genuine desire to achieve a settled state of deliverance and healing.

The **initial stage** processing *phase of recovery* involves a mindset shift to restore the individuals to their pre-trauma state. This is a phase of challenging self-doubt and disabling beliefs emanating from the spirit of trauma.

The **second** stage processing *phase of recovery* consists of advancing the stage processing techniques of deliverance and healing through change and transformation. Fasting is recommended. Fasting requires discipline which develops a resilient mind and produces ketones as an alternative fuel source for the brain.

The third stage processing *phase of recovery* embracing six dimensions of recovery: forgiveness, humility, responsibility, dedication, truthfulness, and honesty. Knowing your identity, position, purpose, and significance in Christ Jesus is essential to seal the recovery process. This phase is marked by your ability to define and understand your purpose and destiny according to the Will of God.

The *fourth stage processing* *phase of recovery* involves new stability in the face of trauma which marks this period of significant growth. Forgiveness heals emotional wounds. Demonstrating gratitude will catapult you into a constant state of mental appreciation. Having gratitude involves the cerebellum—the emotional brain in the temporal lobe—which coordinates thoughts and emotions.

11 | TRAUMA OF CHANGE – STEPS TO REWIRE THE BRAIN

The actions steps describe rewiring the brain when used in tandem with coloring exercises using the templates and the stage processing steps outlined in the Trauma of Change System Model™ will facilitate deliverance from the spirit of trauma, and have a significant impact on trauma wound healing, and recovery.

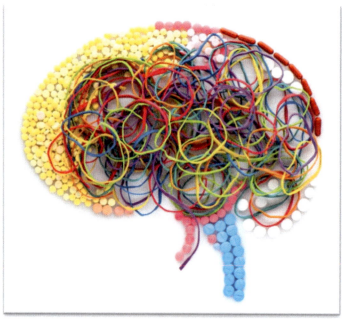

Illustration 8 Source[22]

Creating a New Lifestyle

A habit is the brain's way of helping us simultaneously memorize and repeat the things we regularly do. The ***basal ganglia*** are responsible for habit formation. Habits are sequences of actions that are learned progressively and often performed unconsciously.[23] Habits are crucial for more efficiency for the brain.

Research evidence suggests that the basal ganglia cells are trained to choose behaviors that have been rewarding in the past. The basal ganglia remember the trigger that causes a habit to be repeated.

---

[22] https://stock.adobe.com
[23] "What is Brain Plasticity?" BrainHQ, accessed October 22, 2018, https://www.brainhq.com/brain-resour..."

Creating A New Habit

Each time you establish a new neural pathway, the basal ganglia reward your brain.

It has generally been accepted that habits are formed between 21-30 days. What you do consistently for 30 days can become a habit. Whatever you do for 60 days invariably can become a practice. After 66 days of continuous activity, that habit is going to be as much of a pattern as ever. Whatever you do consistently for 90 consecutive days can become a lifestyle. In other words, after 90 days, the behavior becomes automatic.

The more we purposefully think differently, the easier it becomes to do so. Eventually, the newly established habit becomes the brain's unique way of automatically thinking.

Neuroplasticity

The brain's plasticity, also called neuroplasticity, is behind how habits are formed. Research on brain plasticity and other neuroscientific discoveries has shown that we can increase our neural growth by the actions we take and that connectivity between neurons can change with experiences.[24] The brain's physical composition can alter in response to needs and skill. The cells in your body react to everything that your mind says, which means that if you change the way you look at things, the things you look at will change.

Start to create the life you desire today. ***You can rewire your brain with consistent practice and establish new mental maps and build a habit that will accelerate the formation of new neural growth and brain circuitry in 90 days.***

Habits add consistency and discipline to your life and are essential in you reaching your goals. Encode habits that are beneficial and energy efficient for the brain. Develop memorable goals so that each habit will stick. It will take 30 days to become a habit and 90 days to become a "behavior." To exact **real change**, you must be committed to changing the behavior.

Automatic behavioral engagement can be shut off using the Word of God and will require effort to form new and more effective positive habits. With conviction and concerted effort over the next 90 days, frequently repeated behaviors can become automatic.

Although a habitual action seems so simple and effortless, it typically involves a string of small necessary movements (a process called "chunking"—for example, unlocking the car, getting into it, adjusting the mirrors, securing the seatbelt, and so on). Habits are profoundly ingrained, but the brain's planning centers (prefrontal cortex) can shut them off.

---

[24] Ibid

Practice the 30-/60-/90-Day Term Approach

- **For 30 days**: Establish a goal and implement a hierarchy to establish a habit. Find the key and unlock the door.

- **Over the next 60 days**: Get into the car adjust the mirrors and secure the seatbelt. Practice visualization: where do you want to go? Visualization is critical to prime the brain.

- **At the 90-day juncture**: Drive a new route and create new neural pathways. Use emotions to create what you want. The stronger the feeling is, the stronger the mental map will become. Remember to signal when leaving the curb. When a signaling pattern takes root, a habit has taken shape and breaking it becomes a challenging endeavor.

Committing to a plan to accomplish a goal within 30 days is a good start, but it is still easy to become derailed. **The more you learn how to regulate your emotions** the more in control you will be. If you can keep a new habit for 90 days, the chances of continuing with it for a lifetime are much higher.

There are 10 steps outlined in the Trauma of Change System Model™ on how to rewire your brain and create new and more effective habits and ways to think, feel and respond to the spirit of trauma.

Use a 30-/60-/90-day activity calendar to journal your practice steps. Be intentional. You are 89 days away from making it an automatic reality!

1. Trust in the Word and the Promises of God. Realize that your circumstances have nothing to do with what God has promised you. *"Let this mind be in you which was also in Christ Jesus"* (Phil. 2:5–11, KJV).

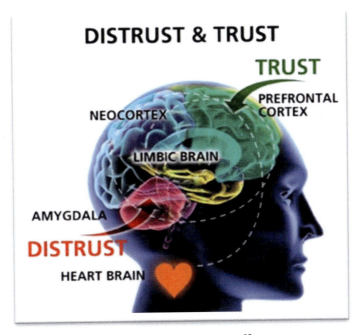

Illustration 9 Source[25]

---

[25] https://www.hrzone.com/engage/managers/the-neuroscience-of-**trust**.

The Trauma of Change System Model™

Trust is part of your brain's default setting. The Anterior Cingulate Cortex (ACC) is the accountant of the brain, organized to assess and reward risk-based decision-making. The ACC is embedded in the prefrontal cortex (PFC). If the actions and beliefs of an individual are not in alignment, it will trigger an alarm to the amygdala. When there is a breach of trust, the brain's conflict detector, the ACC activates the amygdala. Trust and fear are inversely related. Anxiety activates the amygdala. Trust decreases activation of the amygdala. Trust frees up the brain for other activities like creativity, planning and decision-making.

2. Make a quality decision to adopt new and more effective ways to think, feel, and speak to old, disabling beliefs, triggers, and thoughts. Meditate on Romans 12:2: be not conformed to the world but be transformed by the renewing of your mind? You must be intentional because God is intentional.

Illustration 10 Source[26]

3. Write the thoughts that you want to become part of your mental map. Create a script for each day. The act of writing stimulates the limbic system's emotional processing, creativity, and insights.

---

[26] https://www.hrzone.com/engage/managers/the-neuroscience-of-trust

Illustration 11 Source[27]

Decide to Decide

Life is a journey. Each day you can decide how you want to show up and make history. You can choose whether you want to live as a victim or a victorious warrior on the battlefield for the Lord. Adopt the mind of Christ. *"Let this mind be in you, which was also in Christ Jesus"* (Phil. 2:5, KJV).

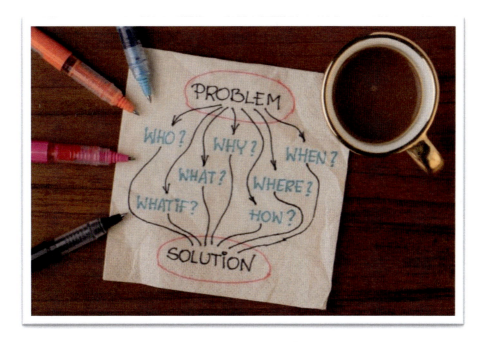

---

[27] https://stock.adobe.com// (under license)

Brain science shows that making decisions reduces worry and anxiety—as well as helping you solve problems. Making decisions includes creating *intentions* and *setting goals* and taking actions. All three are part of the same neural circuitry and engage the prefrontal cortex in a positive way, reducing worry and anxiety.

4. Give yourself permission to rewrite positive narratives and embrace new positive emotions. An emotion is not a thought. Writing deepens neural pathways for learning. *And the Lord answered me, and said, write the vision, and make it plain upon tables, that he may run that readeth it.* (Hab. 2:2 KJV).

An emotion is a reaction to a positive or negative thought. Human emotions can be viewed as the fuel that drives the car. You can't arrive at your point of destiny on an empty fuel tank. Without an authentic emotion, a thought sits in neutral like a car without gas. Conscious and critical thinking will help you to mentally shift and increase the flow of brain connectivity from the left and right brain preventing it from being high-jacked by the amygdala. As referenced in the book *Remembering the Trauma*, the amygdala is wired to detect the threat and how we make decisions, form memories and can encode negative memory into the hippocampus.

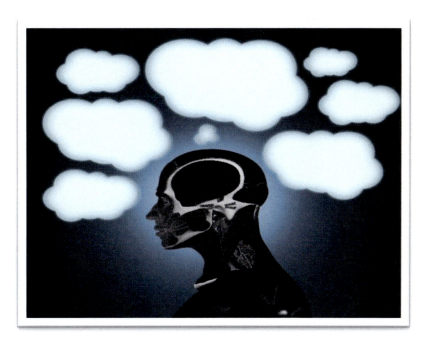

The Trauma of Change System Model™

Workbook Instructions

Record on your phone a narrative in the first person. Imagine you have been selected to write a storyline for prime-time TV and you are the director, producer and lead actor. What is the name of the picture and its opening and closing scenes? Rewrite the trauma experienced with a positive outcome.

_____
_____
_____
_____
_____
_____
_____
_____
_____
_____
_____
_____

5. Give yourself permission to engage in positive thoughts. Gratitude and forgiveness coordinate thoughts and emotions. Gratitude is a constant state of mental appreciation. The benefits of gratitude start with the dopamine system because feeling grateful activates the brain stem region that produces dopamine.

Gratitude involves the cerebellum, the emotional brain, temporal lobe.[28] Gratitude affects your brain at the biological level and boosts the neurotransmitter dopamine.[29]

Be intentional in forgiving those who abused and hurt you. In prayer tell God how grateful you are for His presence, favor and the ability to forgive as he forgives you.

How to Train Your Brain to Stay Positive

Illustration 12 Source[30]

---

[28] https://www.bakadesuyo.com/2015/05/happy-all-the-time/
[29] Ibid
[30] https://stock.adobe.com/ (under license)

Instruction: Write and repeat 8 affirmations daily that you want to become mental map. Your mental map is your perception of what is and will be. The number 8 represents new beginnings.

1. _____
2. _____
3. _____
4. _____
5. _____
6. _____
7. _____
8. _____

6. Visualize your destination. You must see yourself where you want to be before you arrive there. See yourself as delivered, victorious and healed from the spirit of trauma. The process of visualization primes the brain. You can use visualization to create the emotions you want to experience. The stronger the feelings are, the stronger the mental map will be.

When you visualize your intentions, your brain can't tell the difference between what is real or imagined. As you mentally rehearse new affirmations and habits, you strengthen your ability to create them in your life and open portals in your right brain.

"For as he thinks in his heart, so is he" (Prov. 23:7 New King James Version).

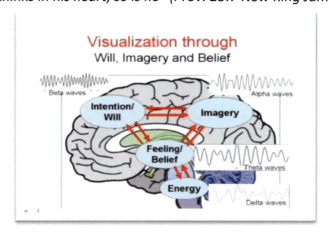

Illustration 13 Source[31]

---

[31] https:// www.newbrainnewworld.com

7. Speak only the truth of God's Word. You are a speaking spirit. Your words matter. Words lack meaning without context. Myles Monroe said, "If the context is wrong the conclusion is also wrong." Your words must line up with the Word of God to effect change in yourself and your life. *"Study to shew thyself approved unto God, a workman that needeth not to be ashamed, rightly dividing the word of truth"* (2 Tim. 2:15, KJV). Study and meditate on scriptures about the change you want to create.

As you align your confession with the Word of God, you will overcome. Our words have the power to destroy and the power to build up (See Proverbs 12:6). The writer of Proverb tells us, *"The tongue has the power of life and death, and those who love it will eat its fruit"* (Prov. 18:21, NIV).

Just as God has come for our words, satan comes for your words as well. Anytime you open your mouth, you are on trial. Words create worlds. *"For by thy words thou shalt be justified, and by thy words, thou shalt be condemned"* (Matt.12:31, KJV).

According to Andrew Newberg, M.D. and Mark Robert Waldman authors of *Words Can Change Your Brain*, "a single word has the power to influence the expression of genes that regulate physical and emotional stress." Positive words, such as "peace" and "love" can alter the expression of genes, strengthening areas in our frontal lobes and promoting the brain's cognitive functioning. Your words propel the motivational centers (right hemisphere) of the brain into action and build resiliency.

8. Practice the thoughts you want to dominate your waking day and dreams. New ideas and experiences create new neural pathways, thought processes, and mental associations. Your mind is renewed as you establish new patterns and practices.

Practice thinking, feeling, visualizing, and acting in alignment with your desired intentions to remove old behaviors and thoughts. When you do this, you give notice to demonic squatters that their time is up by commanding them in the name of Jesus to leave and never return. Repeating new and purposeful actions will become an ingrained and habitual thought process. Be ye transformed by the renewing of your mind. *"And be not conformed to this world: but be ye transformed by the renewing of your mind, that ye may prove what is good, and acceptable, and perfect, will of God"* (Rom. 12:2, KJV).

9. Declare God's Word to override your past. Superimpose the truth of what God says about you over the painful, old, negative memories.

Change requires practicing a new habit. Continually repeat what the Word of God says until it becomes a part of you. Tap into your heavenly language by praying in the Spirit (in tongues). satan cannot discern what you are saying to God as you pray in supernatural tongues. Praying in the Spirit allows the Word of God to have predominance in your mind. As you declare God's Word over you, it will become true to you.

"It is the spirit that quickeneth; the flesh profiteth nothing: the words that I speak unto you, they are spirit, and they are life" (John 6:63, KJV).

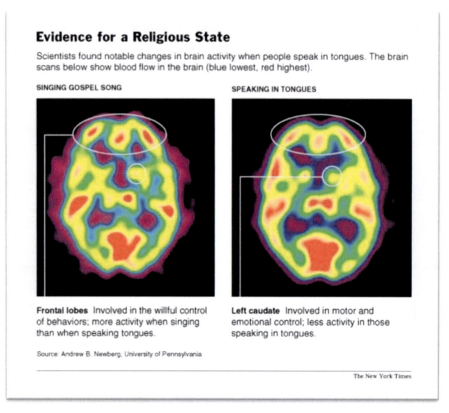

Diagram 1 Source[32]

10. As you meditate and speak the Word of God, allow your heart to release and disallow emotions of anxiety, pain, shame, fear, and guilt. It won't be enough to read and recite the Word of God if you don't believe what it says in your life. Introduce yourself to the new experience of healing and deliverance and the new feelings of peace, confidence, hope, and love.

---

[32] andrewnewberg.com

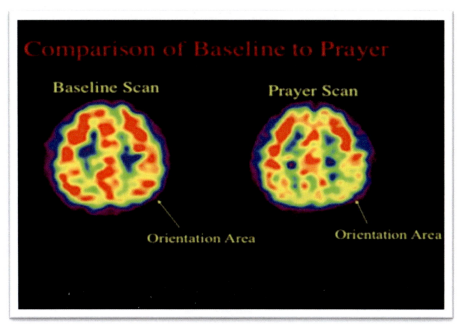

Illustration 14 Source[33]

---
[33] Ibid

12 | PSYCHOLOGICAL PROPERTIES OF COLORS

Color influences the brain, which **leads to an impact on your feelings and senses**. "Color impacts the brain because it can greatly affect our physiology, since it influences **anxiety, pulse, blood flow, and arousal**." Color psychology is the study of hues as a determinant of human behavior. Color influences perceptions that are not obvious, such as the taste of food.

This next segment of the workbook will focus on coloring exercises designed to shift brain connectivity. Building upon the understanding and science of Color Psychology, you will begin the process of restructuring brain circuity with the Word of God and develop new neural pathways.

Illustration 15 Source[34]

There are **six** primary colors in the light spectrum: red, orange, yellow, blue, green, violet. Four of which (red, yellow, blue, green,) relate respectively to the body, the mind, the emotions and the essential balance between these three.[35]

RED | Physical | Body

Its effect is physical; it stimulates us and raises the pulse rate, giving the impression that time is passing faster than it is. It relates to the masculine principle and can activate the "fight or flight" instinct. Red is strong and very basic. Pure red is the most uncomplicated color, with no subtlety. This color evokes physical courage, strength, warmth, energy, basic survival, "fight or flight," **stimulation, masculinity, and excitement.**

---

[34] https://www.funderstanding.com/brain/your-brain-on-color/
[35] ibid

BLUE | Intellectual | Mind

Blue is the color of the mind and is inherently soothing; it affects us mentally, rather than the physical reaction we have to red. Strong blues will stimulate clear thought. Lighter, soft blues will calm the mind and aid concentration; it is serene and mentally calming. It is the color of clear communication. Blue objects do not appear to be as close to us as red ones. This color is the world's most favorite colour.

YELLOW | Emotional

The yellow wavelength is relatively long and essentially stimulating and, therefore, the strongest color, psychologically. The right yellow will lift our spirits and our self-esteem; it is the color of confidence and optimism. Too much of it, or the wrong tone in relation to the other tones in a color scheme, can cause self-esteem to plummet, giving rise to fear and anxiety. Yellow evokes optimism, confidence, self-esteem, extraversion, emotional strength, friendliness, and creativity.

GREEN | Balance

Green strikes the eye in such a way as to require no adjustment whatever and is, therefore, restful. Being in the centre of the spectrum, it is the color of balance—a more important concept than many people realize. This color evokes harmony, balance, refreshment, universal love, rest, restoration, reassurance, environmental awareness, equilibrium, peace.

Coloring Exercises & the Brain

Research on coloring reveals it relaxes the **brain**. When thoughts are focused on a simple activity, your **brain** tends to relax." As you "relax, your brain lowers activity in the amygdala, which is responsible for our fight-or-flight stress response that can lead to inflammation."

The Trauma of Change System Model™

- **Coloring** allows us to switch off our brains from other thoughts and focus only on the moment, helping to alleviate free-floating anxiety.

- Repetition, pattern, and detail prompt positive neurological responses in participants.

- Coloring activity aids in refocusing your attention away from yourself and onto the present-moment event.[36]

- Your brain experiences relief by entering a meditative state.

- Stress and anxiety levels have the potential to be lowered. Negative thoughts are expelled as you take in positivity.

- Concentrating on coloring facilitates the replacement of negative thoughts and images with pleasant ones.[37]

- The prefrontal cortex (PFC) mediates emotional influences on cognitive processes such as decision-making, as well as the cognitive regulation of emotion.

- By removing ourselves as the focal point for our thoughts, we become immersed in what we are doing in the present moment. *(Dr. Scott M. Bea).*

- The practice of adult coloring generates wellness, quietness and stimulates brain areas related to motor skills.

---

[36] Scott M. Bea, Psy.D.,3 Reasons Adult Coloring Can Actually Relax Your Brain retrieved fromhttps://health.clevelandclinic.org/3-reasons-adult-coloring-can-actually-relax-brain/
[37] Dr. Joel Pearson, Adult Coloring Books - wellnessworkdays.com. Retrieved from https://www.wellnessworkdays.com/single-post/2018/04/24/Adult-Coloring-Books

The Trauma of Change System Model™

Workbook Instructions and Activities

*Study the functions of the brain as described fully in the book. Be intentional of how you want to speak to each area of the brain while applying **the steps on how to rewire your brain.***

Today, you are the architect of your brain. There are no limitations placed upon you. Have fun! Tap into the inner child within. Make sure your crayons or color pencils are kept sharpened. You may invite the memory of how the strength of your favorite cartoon resonates with you. Remember you can do all things through Christ which gives you a superpower. Recite the steps to rewire your brain and invite the Holy Spirit to take authority. Do not engage in any other activity while coloring, turn off music, cell phone and avoid any disruption. This is your time—your brain.

Choose colors that resonate with you. *Consider the structure of the brain that you want to rewire more than others. Highlight that area with dominant colors.*

The Trauma of Change System Model™

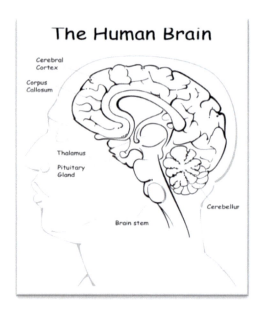

Illustration 16 Source[38]

Instructions: Choose colors that resonate with you. Today, you are the architect of your brain. There are no limitations placed upon you. Remember that God did not give us a spirit of fear, but of power and of love and of self-control. Simultaneously, apply and say out loud the steps outlined to rewire your brain and invite the Holy Spirit to take authority.

Illustration 17 Source[39]

Note: *Conscious and critical thinking will help you to mentally shift and increase the flow of brain connectivity from the left and right brain, preventing it from being high-jacked by the Amygdala. The amygdala is wired to detect a threat, like anxiety, and how we make decisions and form memories. Guilt/shame and pride activate the brain's reward center. Despite their differences, pride, shame, and guilt all activate similar neural circuits including the dorsomedial prefrontal cortex, amygdala, insula, and the nucleus accumbens. Worrying can help calm the limbic system by increasing activity in the medial prefrontal cortex and decreasing activity in the amygdala.*

---

[38] https:// www.jappytopten.com
[39] https://www. adrtoolbox.com

Instruction: Study the brain structures. Consider the areas that you would like to strengthen and to which you would like to have greater access.

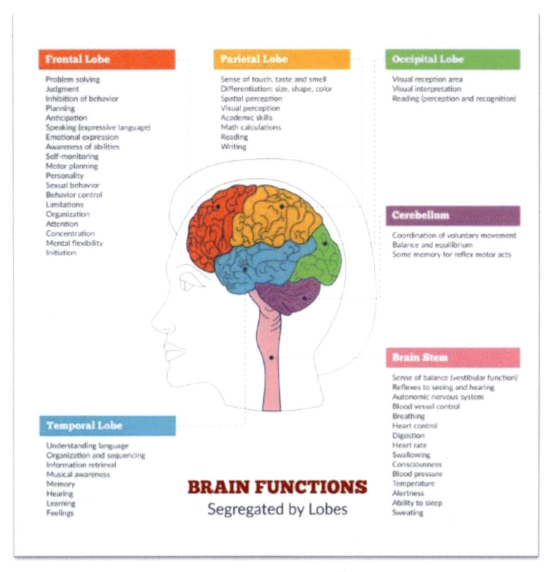

Illustration 18 Source[40]

---
[40] Source: https://www.123rf.com/stock-photo/licensed

The Trauma of Change System Model™

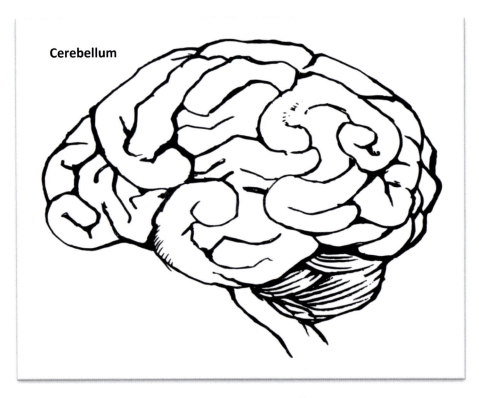

Illustration 19 Source[41]

Instructions:

Color the entire cerebellum. Recall the strength of your favorite cartoon character and how it resonated with you in childhood. Remember, you can do all things through Christ who gives you super strength. Say out loud the steps outlined to rewire your brain and invite the Holy Spirit to take authority.

---

[41] Source: https//www. dreamstimes.com

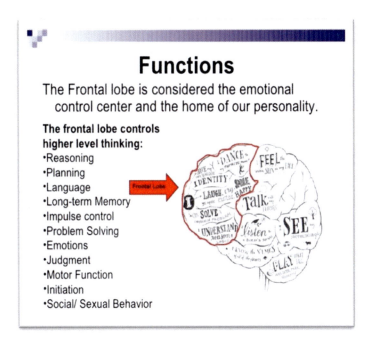

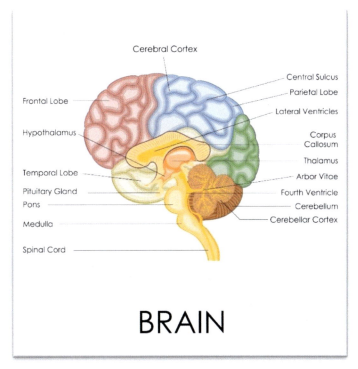

Illustration 20 Source[42]

Instructions:

Consider the functions of the frontal lobe and other structures of the brain. What component would you like to have more influence over and why?

---

[42] https://www.123rf.com/stock-photo/ (under license)

Utilizing the information described about the four lobes of the brain identify and color the lobe that you want to rewire more than others.

Illustration 21 Source[43]

Today, you are the architect of your brain. There are no limitations placed upon you. Have fun! Tap into your inner child. You may invite the memory of how the strength of your favorite cartoon resonates with you. Remember, you can do all things through Christ which gives you super strength. Simultaneously apply and say out loud the steps outlined to rewire your brain and invite the Holy Spirit to take authority.

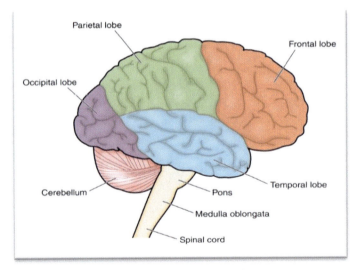

llustration 22 Source[44]

---

[43] Source: cssmith.co
[44] https://stock.adobe.com// (under license)

Instructions:

Color the entire template. In this exercise, you are the CEO of the hippocampus and the amygdala.

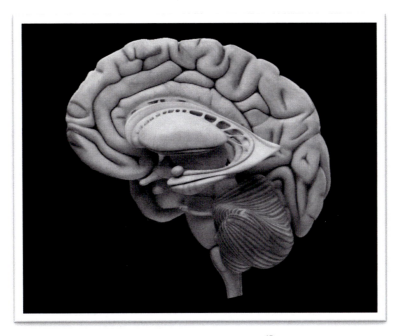

Illustration 25 Source[45]

Instructions: Remember, you can do all things through Christ who gives you super strength. You can to rewire your brain, invite the Holy Spirit to take authority.

What memory do you want the hippocampus to remember most about your ability to become victorious in all things?

1. _____
2. _____
3. _____

---

[45] Source: https://stock.adobe.com// (under license)

The Trauma of Change System Model™

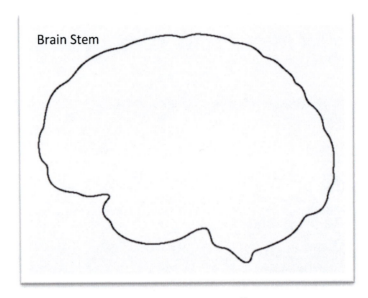

Illustration 26 Source[46]

Instructions:

Apply the steps outlined to rewire your brain and invite the Holy Spirit to take authority.

Instructions:

In this exercise, write the recurring thoughts you want to adopt for the next **30 days.** Color the corresponding structure of the brain involved in developing new habits.

---

[46] Source: cssmith.co

The Trauma of Change System Model™

Use the calendar to record your thoughts about this journey.

1.

2.

3.

Instructions:

Name and insert the emotion that you want the **amygdala** to experience for the next 30, 60, and 90 days. Naming an emotion will affect how it is experienced in the brain.

The Trauma of Change System Model™

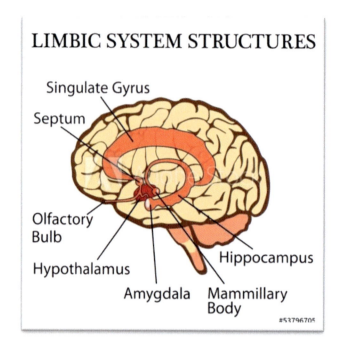

1. 30 Days |
2. 60 Days |
3. 90 Days |

Key: Think only about what you do want to feel. Don't think about any negative emotions that you don't want to feel. You are the architect of your thoughts.

The Trauma of Change System Model™

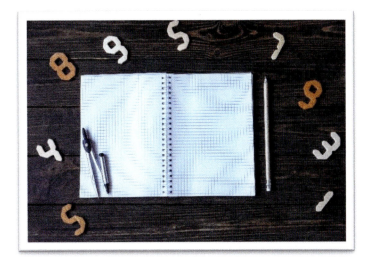

Use the template below to write the recurring thoughts you want to adopt.

Instructions:

In this exercise, write the recurring thoughts in the white spaces that you want to adopt for the next **30 days**.

Use a journal to record your thoughts and feeling about this journey.

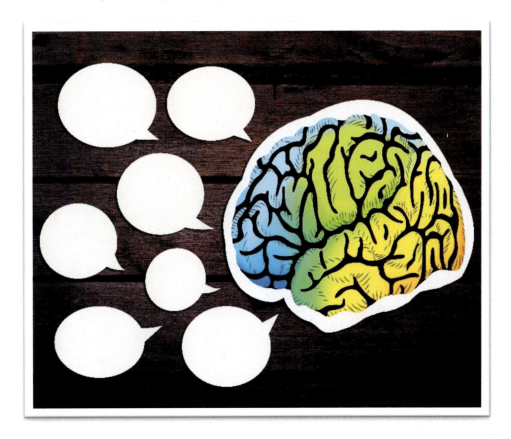

The Trauma of Change System Model™

_____
_____
_____
_____
_____
_____
_____
_____

Instructions:

In this exercise, write the recurring thoughts in the white spaces that you want to adopt for the next **60 days.**

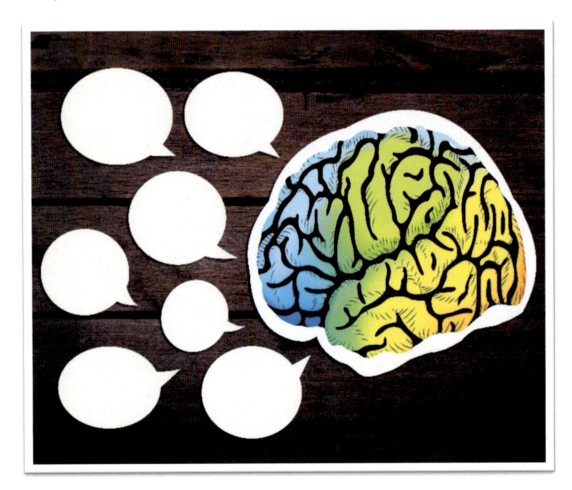

The Trauma of Change System Model™

Use a journal to record your thoughts about this journey.

_____
_____
_____
_____
_____
_____
_____
_____

*Use the template below to write the recurring thoughts you want to adopt for the next **90 days**.*

*Color the corresponding structure of the brain and write the new habits you want to **develop** in the spaces.*

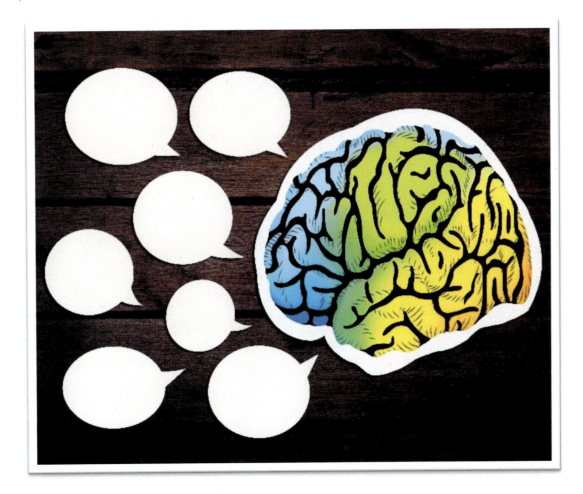

The Trauma of Change System Model™

Use a journal to record your thoughts about this journey.

_____
_____
_____
_____
_____
_____
_____
_____

Instructions:

Using the diagram below as an example, identify and color on blank template the emotions that you would like to predominate your thoughts.

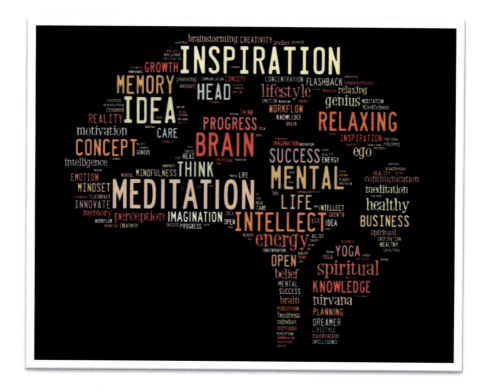

The Trauma of Change System Model™

Color and use the template below to write the top three thoughts as identified in the diagram that you want to predominate throughout the day and even as you sleep.

1.
2.
3.

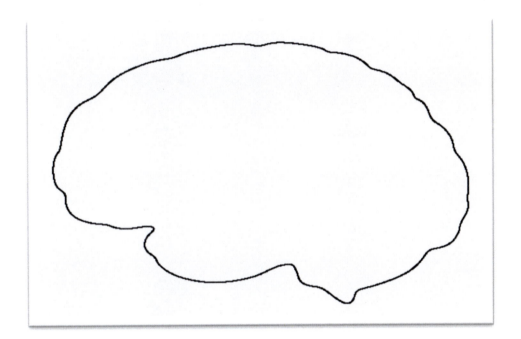

Instruction: Review and use the information on the next page to decide areas of the left and right brain that you want to develop more fully. Use the next template to color the areas and labels the lobes.

The Trauma of Change System Model™

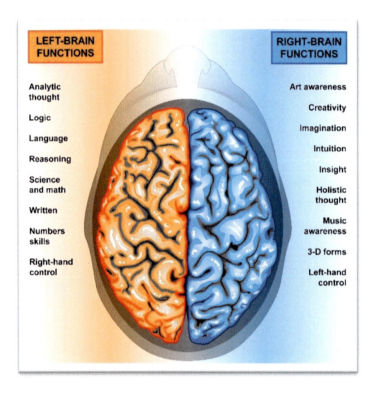

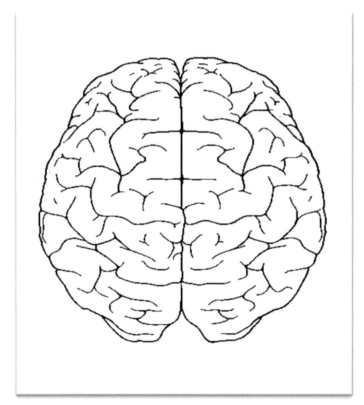

Instruction: Use this template to color the areas that you would like to develop fully.

The Trauma of Change System Model™

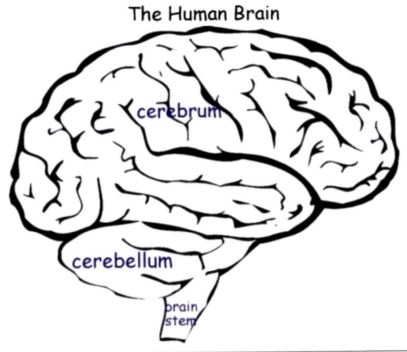

Color the Frontal Lobe red. List some functions the Frontal Lobe controls.
Color the Occipital Lobe yellow. List some functions the Occipital Lobe controls.
Color the Parietal Lobe blue. List some functions the Parietal Lobe controls.
Color the Temporal Lobe green. List some functions the Temporal Lobe controls.
Color the Cerebellum purple. List some functions the Cerebellum controls.

Hint: See diagram of the 4 brain lobes. Make duplicate copies and continue the activities for 90 days.

13 | RESOURCES PAGE

https://www.drabdulsamad.com/anger-effects-brain-body/

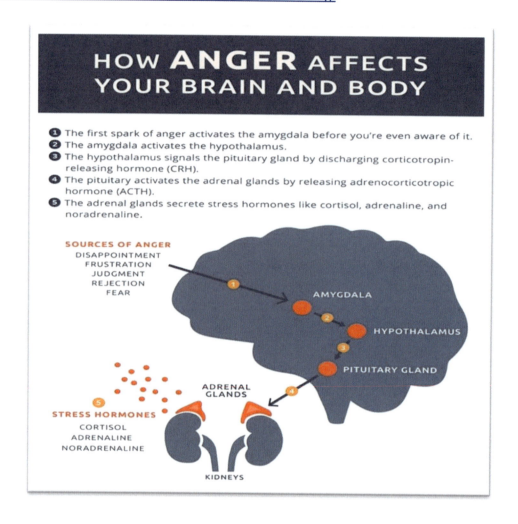

14 | TOC SURVEY QUESTIONNAIRE

1. Of the wound types described in the soul realm, which type(s) resonate most with you? Select all that apply.

    ☐ Penetrating   ☐ Incision   ☐ Abrasion
    ☐ Avulsion   ☐ Perforating   ☐ Puncture

2. On a scale of 1 to 5 (with 5 being the highest rating) how intrusive is the memory of the trauma today. _____

3. On a scale of 1 to 5 (with 5 being the maximum state of repair), what phase of the construction process would you say that you are in? _____

4. Imagine cleaning the debris out of the wound. Is there any object still embedded? If yes, on a scale of 1 to 5 with 5 being the most positive action, how ready are you to take action to remove it? _____

5. Looking back while going forward, how equipped do you feel emotionally on a scale of 1 to 5, to handle wound bleeds? _____

6. What phase of healing would you say that you are in?

    ☐ Homeostasis Phase   ☐ Inflammatory Phase
    ☐ Proliferative Phase   ☐ Remodeling Phase

7. On a scale of 1-5 with five being the highest rated score how likely are you to facilitate the next phase of healing? _____

8. Did you make a confession to accept Jesus Christ as your Lord and Savior during the workbook exercises?   ☐ Yes   ☐ No

To receive a complimentary 10-minute coaching session, return the completed survey and any feedback that you may have to Contact@drreneedcharles.com.

15 | APPENDIX: THE SALVATION CONFESSION

Salvation is the first step towards deliverance. Salvation is an exchange of your trauma for God's healing, deliverance, and freedom. We are born in sin and shaped in iniquity (Psalm 51:5-6).

Jesus experienced every possible trauma on earth. He suffered betrayal (1 Corinthians 11:23); felt shame (Hebrews 12:2); and endured physical and emotional abuse (John 19:1-4). Jesus suffered all these traumas and carried our griefs and sorrows once and for all at the cross (Isaiah 53:4).

Salvation is Available Now

The traumatic events sent by satan were attempts to separate you from God, weaken your body, damage relationships, disrupt healthy thought patterns and drive you into despair.

Perhaps, you have been under the effects of trauma until now. You don't have to suffer from traumatic memories and strongholds. The penalty of sin has already been paid by Jesus.

Healing is immediately available to you if you embrace it. You've already made the decision to choose to heal by reading *Remembering the Trauma* and this companion workbook.

You need not be in a church or religious setting to receive salvation. Let's take the next step of salvation together.

That if thou shalt confess with thy mouth the Lord Jesus, and shalt believe in thine heart that God hath raised him from the dead, thou shalt be saved. For with the heart man believeth unto righteousness, and with the mouth confession is made unto salvation -Romans10: 9-10

Confess Prayer of Salvation

Dear Lord,

I admit that I am a sinner. I have done many things that don't please you. I have lived my life for myself only. I am sorry, and I repent. I ask you to forgive me. I believe that you died on the cross for me, to save me. You did what I could not do for myself. I come to you now and ask you to take control of my life; I give it to you. From this day forward, help me to live every day for you and in a way that pleases you. I love you, Lord, and I thank you that I will spend all eternity with you. Amen.

Short Salvation Prayer

Dear Lord Jesus,

Thank you for dying on the cross for my sin. Please forgive me. Come into my life. I receive You as my Lord and Savior. Now, help me to live for you the rest of this life. In the name of Jesus, I pray. Amen.

16 | BONUS QUIZ

Visit **https://www.webmd.com/brain/rm-quiz-amazing-brain** and take the quiz.

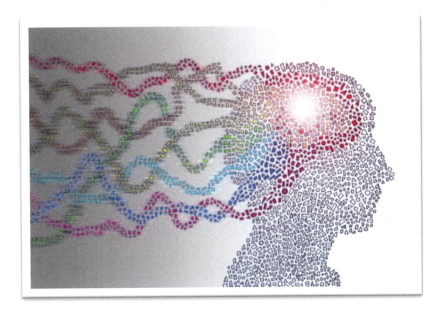

Connect for Next Steps

Services Offered:

- Individual Coaching
- Mastermind Group Participation
- Professional Mentoring

Please send your score sheet and any feedback to Contact@drreneedcharles.com.

The first 100 people will receive a complimentary 10-minute coaching session.

Thank you for your purchase.

Made in the USA
Columbia, SC
19 June 2019